Icebergs, Ice Caps, and Glaciers

By Allan Fowler

Consultants

Linda Cornwell, Learning Resource Consultant,
Indiana Department of Education

Fay Robinson, Child Development Specialist

CP Children's Press®
A Division of Grolier Publishing
New York   London   Hong Kong   Sydney
Danbury, Connecticut

Project Editor: Downing Publishing Services
Designer: Herman Adler Design Group
Photo Researcher: Caroline Anderson

Library of Congress Cataloging-in-Publication Data

Fowler, Allan.
    Icebergs, ice caps, and glaciers / by Allan Fowler.
      p. cm. – (Rookie read-about science)
    Includes index.
    Summary: Describes the characteristics, size, and movement of icebergs,
ice caps, and glaciers.
    ISBN 0-516-20429-7 (lib. bdg.)   0-516-26257-2 (pbk.)
     1. Icebergs—Juvenile literature. 2. Ice caps—Juvenile literature.
    3. Glaciers—Juvenile literature. [1. Icebergs. 2. Ice caps. 3. Glaciers.]
    I. Title. II. Series.
    GB2403.8.F69   1997   96-46951
    551.31–dc21   CIP
                                             AC

The top of a high mountain can get very cold — so cold that snow doesn't melt. The snow piles up, tightly packed — until it turns to ice.

The ice works its way downhill. It follows the easiest path, cutting or deepening a valley.

This river of ice is called a valley glacier.

It is much slower than a river of water.

A glacier might move
no more in a day than
the the size of a single
letter on this page.

Most glaciers move less
than one foot a day.

As it creeps downhill,
the valley glacier changes
the shape of the land.

It picks up boulders, grinds them down, and carries them from one place to another.

Rocks, stones, gravel, sand, and soil are pushed along by the glacier.

When a glacier melts in warmer weather, it leaves great piles of this material behind.

Not all glaciers stay in a valley. Some, known as ice caps, spread out over the land.

One ice cap covers most of the big island of Greenland, close to the North Pole.

These ice caps are more than two miles thick in places.

Icebergs are born where the Greenland and Antarctic ice caps reach the sea.

Huge chunks of ice break off, often with a noise as loud as thunder.

We say that the ice cap is "calving." This is the same word we use when a mother cow has a baby, or calf.

13

The chunks, or icebergs,
then float away.

Ice floats in water, instead of sinking, because ice is lighter than water.

How big is an iceberg? Many of them are several miles long. Some are much larger.

An iceberg bigger than the state of Rhode Island broke off from Antarctica in 1996.

16

An iceberg may stand
above the water higher than
a 30-story building . . . but
that's just the part you can
see, the tip of the iceberg.

The part you don't see —
because it's under water —
is about eight or nine
times as big as the part
you do see.

Hard to believe? Try this at home. Fill a clear glass partway with water. Then put an ice cube in it.

You'll notice that only a little of the cube sticks out of the water. It's the same with icebergs.

Like the ice cube in your glass of water, every iceberg melts — sooner or later.

The iceberg that's as big as Rhode Island is expected to float as much as ten years before melting completely.

Icebergs used to be a
great danger to ships.

One night in 1912, a huge
ocean liner, the *Titanic*,
hit an iceberg in the North
Atlantic Ocean and sank.

21

Ever since then, patrols have been keeping watch for icebergs and warning ships away from them.

No two icebergs are
shaped exactly alike.

An iceberg may remind
you of a storybook castle,
sparkling in the sunlight . . .

or a jagged mountain . . .

or a long white ship.

A giant iceberg is a sight
you will never forget —
as long as you see it from
a safe distance.

But you might see a
glacier up close.

There are even special
buses that let you ride
on top of certain glaciers.

Words You Know

ice and snow

valley

iceberg

ice cap

glacier

calving

31

Index

About the Author

Allan Fowler is a free-lance writer with a background in advertising. Born in New York, he lives in Chicago now and enjoys traveling.

Photo Credits: Comstock: 8, 22, 24; Corbis-Bettmann: 21; Peter Arnold Inc.: 13, 31 bottom right (Norman Benton), 29, 31 bottom left (Helmut Gritscher), 4, 30 bottom (Kim Heacox), 14, 31 top left (Allan Morgan), 7 (Kevin Schafer), 11, 31 top right (Tim Wright), 16 (Bruno P. Zehnder); Photo Researchers: 25 (Robert W. Hernandez), 27 (George Holton); Rigoberto Quinteros: 18; Superstock, Inc.: 3, 23, 26, 30 top; Visuals Unlimited: cover (John Gerlach).